Birds-eye View
From the Floor

Y Wilds

BookLeaf Publishing

India | USA | UK

Presentation by *BookLeaf Publishing*

Web: www.bookleafpub.com

E-mail: info@bookleafpub.com

ISBN: 9789357447027

First edition 2022

ACKNOWLEDGMENTS

I can not express enough thanks to my friends
and family for their support and encouragement.
I couldn't have done this without them. My
deepest gratitudes especially to my cousin,
Jadon Lane for keeping me steady and
reminding me why I do this. Thank you for
being by my side always, you have all my love.
To my best friend, Maleah Hood, for always
cheering me on and holding me up. My partner
in crime for life. And finally to my late
grandmother Laraine Lewis, I wouldn't be here
without her and I do this to make her proud

Ash and Coal

The longer I stand here, my hand limply lingering on the lock, pools of breath fogging up the glass, the more attention I draw to myself. When I can no longer stand listening to myself breathe, listening to the onlookers' silent pleas to know all my secrets, I shift my body weight just so, gracelessly falling out of the jagged doorway. The bitter, wet cold of the night stings my eyes, raising bumps from my fingertips to my spine. I step into the night, letting it envelop me. Secretly, I wish some assailant would come out of the shadows and end all of this incessant back and forth, should I go, should I stay, does it matter; but of course no one comes. And after all, I'm the assailant. I'm the impulsive one with no self-control, lashing out at everything that displeases me, burning every bridge, and rolling every stone along the way.

I drag my hand along the stair railing, cold and smooth. The walk isn't far, maybe only a mile or so. I think of a cigarette but never light one. You'd think I would want one, if not for the last time, but I can't bring myself to spark any kind of fire now, knowing what I know. There is no flame left in me, I'm all smoked out. My shadow dances, flickering as a candle in the wind, but I walk stick straight. Cars pass by the street, their headlights blinding me. My demise calls out to me; clear and melodic like church bells in the distance, my impending downfall pulling me forward. It's cold and I'm sober but I still burn hot, guilt smoldering in my veins like the embers of a drunken mistake. My destination is far too close, my walk is not long enough for me to collect my thoughts. I had hoped the chill of the air would bring me to my senses and make me turn around but the light of the doorway draws me in and I walk with more determination than I ever have. The door handle is cold but I hold it for a moment, breathing in this moment in case it's my last.

It smells like a hospital inside, over sterilized and stripped bare, left empty like a promise. As soon as I open the door remorse floods through me, dousing my uncertainty. That must be why they keep the lights so low and the rooms so small, to make you feel like a white-hot sinner at confessional from the moment you enter. And that's why I'm here after all, to talk about my scolding red truth. I want to talk about the paint peeling from the walls, fast and hard, running away from its home like a child in the night. I want to tell of how the flames licked the ceiling, rising to the heavens with all his worldly possessions in tow. How the smoke filled the room and my lungs. How my head swam with lust and wonder at the destruction, furniture crumpling around me, turning to ash and coal. I want to explain why I stood front and center, laughing and spinning as I threw the fuel around the room. I want to say that I was unable to stop myself, my pain the fuel to this fire. That if I didn't burn it all down then the feelings would never go away and what he did would always haunt me, hanging in the air above my head, heavy and sorrowful. I want to let it out, to finally drag the truth from behind my eyes. To finally bring the words from the back of my mind and off the tip of my tongue. So I figured I'd start simple and small.

"Hi, my name is Leona and I'd like to report an incident of arson."

Fire Starter

"If you can't breathe fire then sometimes you must conjure it."

-Leonna Preston

Always

Trying to remember my past is like looking down a long hallway. There's no real light, never more than the occasional glimmer. The dark is all-encompassing, unwavering. I've blocked out a lot more than I'll ever recover. But I think I know why. It's probably because when I can see, when light breaks through an abyssal crevice of my mind and shines on something once forgotten, I remember what it was actually like. Growing up with you was painful. No other way to put it. More painful than a broken limb.

I sat there quietly listening to the creak of the swing chain. I was small and innocent then, not as clever. My eyes darted around the playground. Not much time left. Maybe only another hour or so. Had to figure it out, make a decision. At first I thought to ask one of the boys. They're stronger so maybe they could just yank my shoulder out of place. No, no that won't work. It's too weird to ask. Ok, what if I throw myself off the jungle gym? I could fall right on my arm. No, that's stupid. But I was desperate. Desperate because I knew.

I knew that when you came to get me you'd ask where my bag was. I had lost another gift. I was forgetful and absent-minded, still am till this day. I knew there had to be a punishment. There was always a punishment. I knew you liked to punish me. You had fun doing it. And I knew not to run or scream or cry. I knew to act like I had fun too. Or there would be more.

So I thought I could break something. And then you'd be too distracted to notice I lost my bag because we'd have to go to the hospital. And then there'd be no punishment. I wanted to break my arm because that would be less painful than being with you.

But I was small and innocent then, not as clever. I never figured out a plan, I was too nervous. Your car pulled up, you beckoned me inside. You immediately noticed the bag. You had a keen sense for those kinds of things, you could smell my mistakes from a mile away. And that was that. I knew what would happen. The same thing that always happened. But if I had known you'd always hurt someone I would've made sure it was always me.

Accidents Happen

There really is no such thing as a mistake.
We do the things we want to until someone else
can see it.

And even when they do, we try to convince
them we didn't mean it.

Crash Into You

Before I got in, I drank. A lot. I ignored my friends' frantic warnings, I ignored my staggered steps and hiccuped goodbyes. I snatched the keys from Sarah, not forgetting the drunken kiss on the cheek. Not because I had a death wish, I did but that wasn't why. Not because I was in a hurry. Just because I liked to drink. I got in. Before I buckled my seat belt, I let myself get distracted when he texted me and forgot all about it. I maintained that exact level of distraction the entire ride home. I paid attention to the way the light from the phone illuminated the whole car, refracting off the rain-splattered windows so pleasantly. I watched my reflection in the mirror, giggled at her bloodshot eyes and dilated pupils. I watched the fog roll over the drenched streets and the condensation rise, losing myself in it. I didn't watch the road, never the road. I snapped back to reality just long enough to swerve for a cat, at least that's what I thought I saw. I pulled the wheel fast and hard, far too hard, a drastic overshot on my part. I spun the car in circles, accidental donuts making the booze slosh in my stomach. The last thing in my mind was that feeling. Floaty like an ocean, now that feeling will always haunt me, for it was the last time I felt free. On my way out I noticed the other car, the one now in much worse shape than mine. Before I broke down crying, choking garbled sighs back hysterically, I made sure to tell the police officer about step one; he was barely interested.

It only hurt a little, my blood painting the steering wheel a muted crimson. My vision spotted and hazy but I could see the other car now on the side of the road. It looked crushed, crunched up like a discarded can. Shit shit shit. I stepped across the scattered glass sparkling from the headlights. If they're dead, do I just run? Before I could get to the car the door swung open. He was fine, or at least fine enough to curse at the top of his lungs. Staring down at the wet curb, and away from him, I was grateful for his screaming. It was a distraction from the thought that my dad would not feel the same gratitude. I wondered only what my punishment would be this time.

Forget Regret

Do you regret it?
And if you do
Be sure in knowing that isn't enough.

Dark Rose

Pink flecks of blush swimming in the air, holding hands with the dust. The smell of hairspray and desperation intertwine into a soft quiet perfume. Girls in their curlers bustled around, palpable nerves tingeing the air a shade of green.

I can remember every detail of the day you called me. Abi, my Rosey. Your voice shaking and fuzzy, the connection spotty. You told me you needed my help, you didn't know what to do, you had taken it too far this time, it was only an accident, you didn't mean to. Said no one could find out, it would ruin competitions for you, it could ruin everything.

You didn't really care that there was a girl now lying face down in front of a vanity mirror. Foam coming out her mouth, frizzes of her hair winding in the reflection. Didn't really care that her family would never hear her laugh again like you do whenever I remind you of this day. Of the story. You didn't care that she probably had more pageants to do too. Probably had dreams, wanted to go to school, wanted to get a new boyfriend or a new car.

But you did seem to care about the blood. You were fixated on the way it pooled in her eyes, red covering a silvery blue, making the faintest lavender. Spilling out of the corners, staining porcelain skin, rouging plump chapped lips.

You were staring.

And it was weird to see you stare at something other than your reflection for once. Confusing even. Made me think that there was something you loved more than the way you look. Made me think maybe you're a little less like mom than I thought. Stronger than her somehow.

Which is why I picked up the mascara you poisoned and put it in my pocket to toss out the window at a truck stop later. Which is why I put my jacket over your shoulders while walking you to the edge of the stage and said "You're gonna kill it." with a laugh. I laughed. And you killed it, first place. And you killed her, or they say an allergic reaction to eye makeup killed her. And no one ever has to know. And that's how we ended our Summer.

Somebody Else

Who you are now is but a shriveling relic of
what I wanted you to be.
Soft, delicate, and lovely
I wanted a pink summer breeze, a clear night
sky.
Wanted the chill of morning air against sweet
flushed skin.
I wanted love when it's new.
Where he could be the warmth and weight in my
bed as the sunlight danced through the blinds
and tiptoed around the room.
But that's the man I wanted you to be
Not who you are
Not even close.

Lullaby

The days were hotter then, melted icee stuck to my fingers, wispy hairs clung to my skin.

He was always so rushed and panicked, like the road would disappear from under the wheels, yellow lines flattened and chewed up by the tires, gray asphalt sucked into the rims and turned to liquid rust.

We clambered into the store and I wandered away; or was sent away, who could recall. Even as a child, I could never tell when I was lost. I never knew when was too far, what was too much, when to turn back.

I looked and looked, wandering in circles. I spun out and around, pacing up and down isles and peeking around corners.

I found them eventually, stumbling upon them by accident. They were in the bikini section. Rosey's flushed cheeks and pouting lips told me everything I needed to know. They were all too familiar. In hindsight, there were so many moments like these. When I knew it was her turn. That my relief was her downfall. And I never did a thing.

We left shortly after, the car racing home, trying to beat the setting sun.

Back in the back seat, we played Patty Cake and I Spy, I tried everything I could to cheer her up. She clung to me like she always did when she was truly upset, not pouting for attention or to be manipulative like she learned from mom much faster than I did.

She got her new bathing suit.

Later that night her face hung low, her big spacey eyes drooped, pooling at her chin in shallow puddles of blue. The freckles on her cheeks floated to the ceiling, trying to reach the sky.

 I sat at the edge of her bed singing her a song. "I love you today as yesterday and tomorrow too. No matter where the sun sets, you'll always be next to me. You'll always be next to me. You'll always be next to me."

Shhh!

I miss the flowers we used to braid in our hair.
The honeysuckles we would drink.
If only those kids knew now, all the secrets we
must keep.

Children of Divorce

The bags under her eyes look like bruises, blues
and green hues intertwine under small gray
dilations that sink to the very back of your mind.
When I hug her she smells like an ashtray,
smokey and forgotten until just the right time.
She's skinnier every time I see her, her tiny
wrists digging into my shoulder blades. Pieces
of platinum come away in my hands. Tufts of
pale thin tangles fall to the sound of beeping
machines

At least they remind us that her heart does still
move, even without dad, even without food,
even without the pills.

Her chart reads Miss Catherine Bradshaw. No
hyphenated name. No mistresses to catch. No
apologies wrapped in silk dust bags. No
lingering glances or sighed goodbyes. No trying
to stay pretty to catch his eyes.

My mother is decaying but at least now she is
free.
I wish I could say the same for Abi.
I wish I could say the same for me.

Mirrors

"Do you think mirrors are really portals?"
" I don't know...I hope so."
" Where would you go?"
" Doesn't matter. Anywhere else."

- Abigail &

Leonna Preston

Versus

Catherine Preston-Bradshaw, 39, Homemaker
John Preston, 43, Paralegal

Catherine

    We live on the dark side of the moon.
Cold, bleak, and covered in shadow,
everything is distantly muffled, like hearing
someone scream for you from above water.
From his creaking office door to the hollow halls
where our kid's once played, I loathe it all now,
more than ever before. I could leave but for
what? What would playing house here, cleaning
and cooking, and putting an ungrateful cheater
through law school have prepared me for? How
will my plastic breasts and nicotine habit, and
ability to stave hunger for days on end grant me
the tools to rebuild the identity I once knew
well? I gave it all up, the hyphen in my name
became the separating line between my identity
and my sacrifice, that is all of what defines me
today. What can I do that hasn't already been
done? And, although I haven't seen anything at
all in this life I'm convinced that looking
through the cobwebbed windows of this house
has made me blind to all that is real anyway,

rendered me unable to take in anything brighter
than this place without wincing as if gazing
straight into the sun. My longing is simply not
enough; forever destined to be a housewife. I
hate it here.

John

I love it here. It's like living on top of
the world, in full perfect view of the sun.
The vivid colors and pleasant scents of the
accomplishment are sweet and familiar like
remembering a song you loved in childhood. I'm
this close. This close to finally passing the bar
and then I'll have it. Perfect wife, perfect kids,
perfect life. I'll change my ways and stay
faithful to make it right to my Cathy. I know all
she cares about is this family and my happiness
so I owe her that much. We've been together
since we were kids, of course a man gets bored.
Of course my eyes wander, and my hands follow
suit. Of course with the lights dimmed and the
walls closed all around I simmer for another like
I once did for her in the back of my father's car.
But what a pity to be like him, again I am his
same. Just as he deceived my mother I hide my
indiscretion from my lover. But only if to protect
her, she's delicate that way. Who I am is my own
man, my life mine to choose. If I were to stop
now I could be nothing like him. As men,

however, we share afflictions, passed down for
generations, curses remain unbroken. Love
remains lost. I can try harder though. Stop
hurting all of them, all at once. I stopped with
Leonna, I can stop with Abi too. Then they'll
see, it can be perfect here.

Nostalgia is a Disease

Perfection isn't real, the way nostalgia is a disease.
Desire is haunting that way, staining everything it touches, lingering the air long after you're gone.
I still smell your longing on my clothes, in my hair. It's been years but it's still there.
I can't imagine what she must feel like.
How she must choke on it every time you look her way.
How much it suffocates her while she's trying to sleep, your thoughts violating her even when you're out of reach.
How desperate she must be for fresh air, even when you're not there.

Lovelost

I guess you could say I loved you. The same way one loves a cigarette. A vicious vice, curling around my fingers, kissing my lips, licking my throat. Gray and choking, blacking my lungs. Just as bruised and battered as my mascaraed eyes, streaming black and inky, leaving stains on my skin.

But I guess you could say I loved you. I surely let you do whatever you wanted to. Blacken my eyes, red my lips, purple and blue the curves of my hips. At first you said sorry but eventually you stopped. Who was I to make you pretend to be something you're not? A leopard never changes his spots. But God did I try to change you. Break you, in ways I knew only I could do. And still, I ended up in a cast. You never so much as bought flowers but promised last time would be the last.

Yes, I loved you. And I still do.
But loving you didn't stop me.

Goodbye

Running away is much easier than it looks.
You practice a million times before it happens.
The trick is making sure no one notices that
you're gone.

To Abi

We got our matching tattoos.
Yours a thorn, mine a rose.
We promised to protect each other. To always
stick together.
I didn't then, I was such a coward.
But eventually, I did keep that promise.

[Untitled]

One day you wake up and you know what you've always known.

La Fin

The headlights drowned out the grandeur of the house. Bathed in over-exposed white it stood too big, looming over me like an elaborate prison. Or maybe I just breathed in too much snow on my way there. I checked my reflection one last time for any hints of white or red on my nose. The keys were out of the ignition, laying on my lap. I could never just go in, even then. I always just sat there contemplating turning back, going home or to the bar or to the nearest cliff I could take a swan dive from. The cold was wet and bitter, by the time I reached the door my hands already stung. The key was under the rock like it always was, that was the only thing left how it used to be.

Inside was dark, the Christmas tree the only thing lighting up the living room. I was surprised they even put up a Christmas tree without mom around.

Then I thought I heard a whimper.

It came from the back of the house. A cold clammy panic covered my whole body. Shakily, carefully, I crept down the hall hissing for her like a trapped snake. I didn't want to believe what I already knew, but the closer I got the more I could hear him.

My memories flashed, hitting me like bullets that burst into flame. His gruff grunts, his scruffy beard against my tiny thighs. Waves of nausea rocked through me, leaving a hollow pit in their wake. I was eight years old again.

Leaning against the office door at the edge of the hall, I cracked it open. Abi's lilac skirt was bunched up around her thighs. That was the first and only thing I noticed, my eyes stuck in place. I was barely even there, like a faint whisper of myself, already forgotten. In my peripheral I could see his legs between hers. Back and forth, back and forth. Somewhere in a distant part of my mind, I thought, it sounds like the seesaw we had when we were kids. Back when it was my turn. With its red chipped paint and rusty handle. We loved it. We were happy then. Squeak, squeak, squeak, squeak. It wasn't until I noticed her sniffling. Over my father's shoulder Abi had finally noticed me, both of us frozen in place. Little icebergs melting apart. He was burning through us. My eyes locked on Abi's, hers tearful and meek, mine dry with rage. As if breaking from a trance, he finally realized Abi was starring. Reluctantly, he followed her eye line. Dad's turn to be frozen.

I completely snapped. Stretched too long, too thin. There was no coming back. I told her to leave. It wasn't a request, she knew that. She tried to protest and I knew she would try to interrupt as if this could be explained away. I pointed out of the door behind me. I didn't know what I would do yet, but whatever it was I didn't want her to see it. Of course, he did try to make excuses while awkwardly pulling up his pants. As if he could cover it up. My sister hopped off the desk like she had to get away before hearing his lies. The same lies he had been telling for years. She squeezed my shoulder on the way out, so softly. I got a good look at her up close. She looked just like me when I was younger. My little sister and her silent thank you.

The rest is a bit of a blur. At first I enjoyed listening to him stammer. I had never seen him anything less than composed. I had never been the aggressor between the two of us. I told him not to bother lying. But he just wouldn't stop talking. I was constantly keeping myself from screaming. Trying to hold it in, afraid that if I screamed I'd lose all control. I needed control for once. I cleared the distance between us slowly, deliberately then. He started backing up, knees buckling on the edge of his desk.

My grin was sky-high, kissing the
ceiling, it hurt my cheeks. I seemed just like
him. I hit him. With the wine glass sitting on his
desk. Over and over and over again. Then I knelt
to the ground and laid my head on his chest, the
same way I used to when we were kids on movie
night. He was still breathing. They were jagged,
shallow breaths but they were there. I went to
leave, I didn't care if he ever got up again.

The darkness of the house felt different
when I left his office. Heavier, more permanent,
more real. Maybe it was present in me then,
made me a shadow of myself. Maybe that's why
I thought I had to get rid of the whole thing.
Only fire could do it, cleanse away all the fear
Abi, mom, and I felt for years at hands of one
man. I had to pour the vodka I found in the
kitchen all over the counter and then the floor. I
had to put the spray in the microwave and let it
spin. I had to sit in the living room and wait.
Because if I didn't see flames I wouldn't know it
was true. Wouldn't know I had really fixed him,
by erasing him. So I basked in it for a while.
And then I left. I saw Abi's car was gone.

The next day she called to thank me and
said dad was alive and in the hospital. I figured I
better confess before he got the chance to. He

didn't deserve to tell the story, I had to beat him
to it. I had to beat him one last time.

I'm Sorry

"I don't regret what I've done, I only regret not doing it sooner."

-Leonna Preston

Y.

www.ingramcontent.com/pod-product-compliance
Lightning Source LLC
LaVergne TN
LVHW010948200726
843509LV00013B/2322